MARKED

Understanding and Unraveling
The Call Of God On Your Life

By Faith C. Wokoma, Psy.D

ISBN-13: 978-1724802316

Contents

Acknowledgements

To my mom, who was marked before I was ever marked. I want to thank you for the price you paid to carry me, to raise me up in the fear of the Lord. For teaching me to love God and how to worship. For allowing me to walk passionately with him even from an early age, for releasing me into the work of the kingdom as early as 17 with no hesitation. For the Bible stories and songs every night, for choosing spirit filled churches and those you know would be a blessing to your children. For your faith and faithfulness, and example of steadfastness with God. For the anointing to pray and teach and for extending those generational blessings. You are worthy of double honor. This one is for you!

Are You Marked by God?

Introduction

What does that even mean? In a nutshell, it means you have been set apart for something amazing. While every believer has been set apart for good works (Ephesians 2:10), there are some people who have been set apart to do unique and extraordinary things in their walk with God and service to God. Remember the children of Israel in Exodus 12:7? The angel of God came and marked their doors to protect them from the angel of death. 2 Timothy 2:20 says, "In a large house there are articles not only of gold and silver, but also of wood and clay; some are for special purposes and some for common use."

While God uses all those who are called by his name, the world readily identifies certain people as unique from birth. People and things are usually marked to tell them apart from the other people and things. The ones marked are separated from the rest of the bunch. And by marked, I mean set apart for a specific work. I am not saying some people are better than others, what I am simply saying is some people's journey will look very different from the majority of people and usually that is because God has called them to a specific work. The journey to that thing is what sets them apart and qualifies them to do something extraordinary with their life. There are many who are called and marked but lack the training and information to fully manifest the greatness they were made for. My desire in writing this book is to give you some insight into the temperaments, makeup, and journey of someone who is called and marked by God. The book has several lists, and even some homework, to help you gain clarity and insight about who you are, why you have gone through or experienced what you have experienced and who you are becoming.

CHAPTER 1

The Traits and Characteristics of Marked People

I have been a psychologist for about ten years and a minister of the gospel for fifteen years. In my experience, I have ran into many beautiful souls at different stages in their life where it has been clear that they were "marked" or set apart for something extraordinary. Telltale marks of their uniqueness is embedded in their story, their struggles, their pain, their triumph. From the womb to the day the walk in their greatness, signs are unfolding. The first list in the book are the twenty-two signs I have observed that signal someone is marked for something extraordinary.

I will assume you are reading this book because deep down inside you know you are marked or maybe you are not sure but people have said you are. Either way, I believe as you will find the language for your experience and healing for your journey as you read.

Attacks In The Womb And The Early Years

As we have mentioned, the marking on your life probably emerged very early. The enemy seeks to destroy you even before you are born. Many people who are marked or set apart for service experience things like nearly being aborted or their mother nearly dying while carrying them. The enemy does not know everything about you, but he can often sense when there is something unique on your life. Attempts to destroy you early in the womb are a clear indication that you are marked. Before I go on, I am not going to assume everyone knows who I am referring to when I say enemy. I believe we are all made in the image of God, that His son Jesus died so you do not have to live a life of mediocrity or pain or sin. According to scripture, God has an enemy and he is also our enemy. He is called the devil. From the time he was banished out of heaven until now, his job is to not only pull us away from a relationship with God our Father, but to kill us physically, emotionally or spiritually, to steal our identity and cause us to live a life that is lived based on the expectations of others, and to destroy the original plan God has for us. In Jeremiah 1:5, God speaks to a young prophet in his teens named Jeremiah and tells him, "Before I started to put you together in your mother, I knew you. Before you were born, I set you apart as holy. I chose you to speak to the nations for Me."

That same promise is over your life. You have already been set apart. You are already known by your maker. He has already chosen you. The process of being marked is learning to believe that and discover what it is we have been set apart for. The enemy knows this, so his plan is to deceive you out of this great promise.

If the enemy cannot destroy you in the womb, you may have near death moments at birth things like being born with a cord around your neck, being born prematurely, or some other unforeseen challenge. The enemy's attempts to kill you physically do not end at birth. Some experience a childhood marked by sickness, poverty, physical abuse, and/or neglect. A lot of these issues may be due to the environment we were born in, poor decision making by our parents or forefathers, or a result of ignorance—not having enough information. Either way, the enemy looks in our history or environment and our family for things he can use against us even before we are born. Once again, he does not know all that God has put in you, but he surely does not want you to be around to discover it.

For some, the attacks may not be physical but more emotional. Your mother may suffer with anxiety and depression which may attach to you from the womb, causing you to be extremely anxious or to struggle with insecurity and mental and emotional issues. You may have had an alcoholic or abusive parent waiting for you when you exited the womb, making your early years a living hell. Others suffer with low self-esteem, things that are meant to break your soul like sexual abuse or physical abuse. All of these things are early clues that God has great plans for your life.

A lot of our early psychological and emotional experiences impact who we believe we are and what we become. Many marked people struggle with abandonment and rejection. We will discuss how to overcome that as we go.

You Were A Unique Child

Even as a small child you were unique. You thought differently, had a vivid imagination, spent time alone, or were wise beyond your age.

Marked children tend to be unique even from the time they are born. They can be seen as overly social, creative, smart, and energetic. On the other end of the spectrum, they can be seen as isolative. They may have difficulty making friends or struggle with rejection. Marked children are often seen as wiser than their age and can often be referred to as an "old soul." There is a grace and a uniqueness about these children. They're often fascinating, and people will say things like, "You're going to change the world" or "There is something unique about you." As amazing as these words may be, this can be a very difficult time for a young child or teen who does not fully understand their uniqueness is a gift not a curse. Many older marked people may have struggled with bullying, perfectionism or isolation growing up because they did not understand or manage their difference. If you are reading this and you are a parent of a marked child, it is your job to help them understand their uniqueness but also encourage them to be normal children. We have seen many actors, actress and icons such as Michael Jackson, who at a very young age was clearly gifted or marked, thrust into the limelight and subsequently, a world beyond them. Often times, this can be traumatic. We saw in Michael's life how often he longed for a place of safety which he eventually created and named Never Never Land for his twelve-year-old self. It is important that when we recognize a child's uniqueness, we surround them with support to grow gracefully into their greatness.

You Have A Fascination For The Supernatural Or For The Things Of God

Marked children often have an unexplainable love for God , even if they do not know God.

No matter the culture or background, marked people are often interested and involved in the supernatural. I believe the wiring for something greater than yourself often makes you hungry for something bigger than you. For many marked people, God's hand is on their life even when they don't know Him. God is and has always been pursuing you. You will find many people who are marked with great purpose love God. I have a friend who grew up as a Hindu, but God would visit her and later led her to Jesus through a vision. The goal is not just to know God but to encounter Jesus because part of being marked is making the name of Jesus known in the earth. When you are marked, you may be the only one who went to church while your parents stayed home. You may have had a desire to go to prayer meetings when no one else was around. Marked people specifically love the presence of God, love to be where He is. They connect to the unseen, to what others don't. This is a good thing, but it can also be negative because during this time the occult often searches out these children. They know they are unique. If the child or even adult does not know the difference, they may spend years in New Age or occultic practices hoping to connect to a higher being when God the Father and Jesus the Son have been there all along.

Love Connecting To God Through Worship And Prayer

Most marked people have a streak of creative genius in them. Whether it's in the sciences, the arts or spiritual things, there is a part of greatness that is connected to creativity. Even resiliency is connected to creativity, being hopeful is connected to creativity, so it's no wonder marked people are passionate about worship and prayer. As I previously mentioned, they hunger for the supernatural. Many understand their source of passion, creativity and power comes from something bigger than them. I know you're wondering how this is connected to creativity. Worship and prayer are connected to the same area in the brain in which creativity is birthed. There is something about freedom and liberty in worship that allows our minds to be open and to expand so we are able to think beyond boundaries and limitations and connect to something much higher than ourselves. Creatives, Thinkers, Pioneers, Builders are always looking for inspiration that is bigger than themselves. They somehow can connect to the bigger picture despite what is standing right in front of them. I have found those that are spiritually marked have a huge passion for the presence of God, the things of God, and for worship.

The Fight For Normalcy

Growing up, trying to be normal never worked. Even when you fit in, you always stood out.

I have found that people who are marked know they are different. Many will try to be "normal" in an effort to not have to deal with their difference. However, their difference will pull them out. One that is marked by God may try to hide in class but always gets picked to lead. May try to do the same things everyone else is doing but always gets caught. The important thing to understand is there is no real normal. What the world deems as normal is abnormal in the kingdom of God. We will discuss this more when we talk about identity and authenticity, but if you have had one or more nights in which you cried out to God, "JUST MAKE YOU NORMAL," this is a clue that you have been marked. We have all been there.

The enemy lies to marked ones because he wants you to believe what you see is what is applauded in heaven, but it is the things that are unseen, the things that seem foolish on the outside that are applauded.

The Black Sheep Syndrome

People don't get you and, often times, that includes your family. When people are unique or carry something extraordinary, they are often ostracized. Unfortunately, sometimes family members are the culprit. Many people who carry a unique gifting or calling often feel misunderstood by their family. They may be talked about or ridiculed by siblings and parents. The black sheep syndrome is the idea that there is no one else like them and sometimes your own family may tell you that and may exclude you or make you feel like something is wrong with you. I have seen cases in which the enemy used one's own parents to beat them or tell them things like, "I wish you had never been born," or rally the rest of their family against them. Remember, it is not anything you have done but who you are. When Jesus was born, Herod heard a king had been born and sent out spies, even the wise men, to find him. Often the enemy will use people close to you to destroy you. Many people have said things like, "I think I was born into the wrong family," just because they are so different from everyone else around them. The enemy may try and use this to make you feel like there is something wrong with you, but the truth is you were made to stand out and change the world. Think of Joseph, his family threw him into a pit and left him for dead. From the depths of a prison to his ascent to Potiphar's house, when famine struck the land, he became the means to salvation for the same family that ridiculed and betrayed him. I believe many of you will be able to say what Joseph said to his brother in Genesis 50:20, "As for you, what you intended against me for evil, God intended for good, in order to accomplish a day like this—to preserve the lives of many people." It is all working out together for your good.

They Are A Prophecy Magnate

Marked people attract seers and hearers from every background. They will find many people will come to them or their parents and speak about the greatness that is in them.

Marked people are prophecy magnets. I have a friend who was prophesied to while he was in the womb by Hindu monks of his greatness. The monks came to his mother and told her of his future. We spoke about the occult above, but many times, psychics, witches, and New Agers, as well as spirit filled believers can sense and see greatness on a person. That's why they attract people from all walks of life. Unfortunately, not every person has good intentions in sharing those words. Everyone can sense greatness and can identify those who are marked by God even if they grow up in a none Christian home. Teachers and random people on the street may say things like, "You are unique," You are special," or "There is something about your life."

The world is aware of who the unique ones are, sometimes even when the marked person is not. God will have it that you continually get words of affirmation and direction to help lead you in the direction He has planned for you.

Things That Are Easier For Others Are Hard For You.

For some marked people, the trouble starts early. You hear stories about difficulties learning to talk or walk or challenges with school with and learning or processing information. It seems like for some marked people things that flow with ease for others may take more effort on their part or may seem nearly impossible. Even if a marked person do not who they are, the enemy is constantly conspiring to discourage them or to take them out. Your ability to persevere in hardships allows you to be relentless and resilient.

Many people who are marked have great resilience. Resilience is the ability to bounce back from difficult circumstances. Marked ones are able to fight through circumstances and situations that would have killed most people.

Those who are marked may also struggle with finances or finishing projects such as college. They may say things like, "I always have to fight for everything" or "Why are things so hard for me?" Here is some encouragement. It will not always be like that. The more you grow into your purpose and understand the authority you have in helping God shape your life, you will no longer feel like a victim who is always on the receiving end. You will begin to feel powerful, like one who can walk with God in shaping their life.

They Can Never Do What Everyone Else Is Doing

Because of God's hand on their lives, marked people often live with stronger levels of conviction. Many may experience a stronger sense of guilt than their counterparts who do not feel guilty about certain things. They may also try and act like their counterparts and get in trouble, while it seems others are getting away with doing as they wish. For marked ones, it may seem like punishment, especially when you are growing up but the truth is, it is a protective factor. God is trying to keep you from destroying yourself and what He has put in you. Getting caught easily or high levels of conviction are really a protection not a punishment.

Marked ones have a strong conviction even when they do not want to do the right thing. Many may run or try to hide from this thing they are made for but somehow still find themselves eventually running towards what is right.

As I have mentioned before, marked people struggle with wanting to belong and wanting to be normal. Often times, they will rebel against systems that are in place to propel them into their destinies. However, due to the fact that God's hand is on them even in seasons of rebellion, they know that what they are doing is wrong and not what God intended for them to do. They may try to rebel and even stay in that place that is the total opposite of who they were made to be, but deep down they know they are made for something bigger than what they have settled for.

They Have A Different Perspective On Life

Every marked person has a prophetic gift, whether they know it or not. Many just know things, many have great glimpses and ideas about the future, many are seen as being wise far beyond their age, and because of the prophetic nature of a marked person, they see the world differently. Sometimes they see all the good and some others see the negative. Marked people have a clear idea of how to change the world. They understand the word of the world. They often "know" these things but are not sure why others do not know or see those things as well. A strong gift of discernment for marked people allows them to know things about people, situations that others may not be able to see or comprehend. In the following chapters, I will illuminate how God communicates and how to know His voice.

Seen As Zealous Or Too Passionate

Marked people, especially those called to the body of Christ, often struggle with the opinions of others. Often times people have said things like too deep, passionate or even too zealous. Marked people tend to have supernatural faith and a supernatural hunger for the things of God, like the 12-year-old Jesus in the temple, they tend to have wisdom and power beyond their age which often intimidates leaders and others who are not walking with as much passion or purpose. Marked ones often struggle with feeling like they need to dumb themselves down because they are "too much" or they are "too intense." The list of "toos" never stops. There are seasons when a marked person may need to slow down. Oftentimes, marked people tend to have addictive personalities. Once their heart is set on something, nothing will stop them. If the person is not fully processed or mature, this can cause issues in their pursuit or in their relationships. The joy of being a marked person is learning how to master and control your zeal and passion. The enemy wants to wipe out the passion, but your job is to learn how to properly carry it so you can accomplish what God has called you to do.

Seasons Of Loneliness

Being marked is interesting because several things are happening at once. God wants you to know you are loved and belong to Him, so often people will reject you and cause you to walk alone. These seasons are not to break you. These seasons are to draw you closer to God. Some marked ones love people so much they begin to get their validation from people. Others long to please people or walk in fear of them to the point that God calls the marked one to Himself. The journey of the "wilderness" or season of being set apart works best when a person understands they are marked and what God is trying to do. However, due to the lack of teaching, many go through wilderness seasons with very little clarity and a lot of pain. I am praying this book helps bring insight to the process. God allows us to be alone so we can learn to lean on Him, gain our confidence from Him and become like Him.

They Dream BIG Dreams

Marked ones are dreamers, not only at night but also during the day. Often, marked ones are seen as those whose dreams are bigger than most. Marked ones are often the ones caught daydreaming in class, pretending they are in a different time and space. What they see for their life and the world around them is bigger and brighter than what they are seeing in the natural realm. Joseph was one such dreamer. He was marked by God and haunted by his dreams. He knew what he had seen, but the process of manifestation nearly killed him. Marked ones have to contend for their dreams and their visions even in the face of opposition. Many times a marked one may feel like they are losing their mind because what they see is so much bigger than their resources, education or sphere of influence.

There is always a place of faith in a marked person's life where God teaches you that His words and what you have seen and heard for the future is much more important than what is happening in the present. The dreamer can nearly taste it or touch it, yet the reality seems far off.

The dreamer may even try to bury the dream, but like a perennial, it springs back up season after season. Marked ones are made for big things, and these big dreams often must take root in our own hearts before we see them in reality. The enemy is the thief of dreams, however, the Lord is the maker of them. A dream does not die until the dreamer has died. So keep dreaming no matter how crazy, wild, or unimaginable they may be. The Dreamweaver planted your dreams inside of you.

Emotional And Psychological Breakdowns

Several factors cause marked ones to struggle with their emotions. One is mentioned above. Seeing and knowing something much bigger than yourself can cause a marked one to feel like they are losing their mind. Due to the prophetic nature of marked ones, explaining their dreams and experiences to other people may feel like something akin to a psychological disorder. There is a group of marked ones who often feel the emotions and pain of other people. These people have a high level of discernment, and when a person is unaware of this gif, they assume all the emotions they are feeling are theirs. This causes them to be **labile** which simply means their mood swings from highs to lows and back and forth. Other marked ones, due to the nature of the traumas they've experienced or the hardships of their life, may develop disorders such as Post Traumatic Stress Disorder or Major Depression. Why are marked ones targeted? We have said this many times, but we must understand that these dreams, passions, and things we know we were made for are not just for us or from us. They are from God for people around us. When you think of the many gifts that have walked the face of the earth — Einstein, Donatello, Sojourner Truth, Whitney Houston, Nelson Mandela, Mahatma Gandhi, to name a few — they all have deposited something significant for the world to share. What is in you is a threat to the kingdom of darkness and one way the enemy discredits you is to cause you to struggle mentally or think you have lost your way. I have found that once people find the purpose in their pain, they can begin the process of healing. However, there are some who end up with a diagnosis that changes their trajectory of their life.

Remember just because you do not fully know what is on your life does not mean the enemy doesn't. The opposition he comes after you with is for where you are going and the impact you are supposed to make, not who you are right now. The best thing to do is see a counselor, speak about what you have been through, get on medication if you have too. Get healed, go through deliverance and find a community that can support you.

Infectious Hope And Faith

With everything that a marked person goes through, you would think many of them would have a gloomy outlook on life, but it is often the opposite. One trait I have observed concerning marked ones is their infectious hope and faith. Many people who are marked always see the glass half-full no matter what is presented to them. The innovators, the thinkers, the creatives that we admire today all have one thing in common. They did not give up! Michael Jordan, one of the greatest basketball players that has ever played the game, did not make his eigth grade basketball team. Mark Zuckerberg, who started Facebook, had several challenges in the beginning. I believe God wires marked ones to persevere through opposition. It is what makes them marked. In areas where others have been discouraged, marked ones somehow find the faith and belief that it can be done. If you're going to change the world, you have to be able to have hope. It is the trademark of a marked person.

Born Before Their Time

Marked people are not limited to the generation, culture or time they're born in. A trait of a marked person is their ability to see beyond their own culture. They love people who are different from them. They often consider those outside their immediate sphere of influence and surroundings. They often see beyond their generation and their time. Marked people are often criticized and misunderstood in the season or generation they are born in because they are ahead of their time. For example, in his book, *1984*, prophetic writer George Orwell wrote about things that seemed foreign at that the time, but we are seeing them in our present day. He was ahead of his time. Marked people are seers that can often see the future and begin to create it. Many experience ridicule for this amazing gift while alive and celebrated for their genius generations later. This can cause a lot of emotional trouble because you may be ostracized and or criticized for losing your mind. That's why marked ones need support systems. They need people who can give them meaning and language for their experiences to help normalize what is happening in their life. Most artists like Leonardo da Vinci and prophets like Martin Luther King were not really valued or understood until after their deaths.

They Love People And Often Forgive Easily

Marked ones often have a huge passion for humanity and for those around them. While many go through heartbreak and hurt from family members and peers, they have an ability to forgive easily. Continued hurt can damage the soul of a marked person which may cause them to close up and inhibit their ability to interact or relate to others. Being misunderstood, being born before their time, or a marked one's uniqueness are other factors that can cause them not to love people well. Generally speaking, marked ones have a passion for people and they easily forgive. This is directly attributed to their resilience. You cannot be resilient if you continuously hold on to the past and things that have been done to you. You must be able to forgive and let things go in order to keep moving forward. In order to not die or be closed off from the future, captured in a place of unforgiveness, it is of utmost importance for a marked one to forgive. Not only does unforgiveness contaminate your gift, marked ones must be processed in order to make sure the gift they give the world is pure. We have seen many marked ones with pain in their heart and what they have released has not been a pure offering to the Lord.

Natural Born Leaders

Marked ones are usually the first volunteer, the ones who always raise their hands. They are willing to lead when others are not. People who are marked for greatness are forerunners. They tend to go ahead of the pack and are willing to take one for the team. They are focused and have tough skin. They're often the ones to take risks when no one else is taking risks. They are often the ones who are willing to be ridiculed instead of sitting there not saying or doing anything. They are leaders who stand up for the voiceless. They are champions of those that cannot fight for themselves. They would rather try to do something they have never done than remain in a place of safety. Leadership in a marked one appears in many forms, personal leadership over your own life or leading a business, ministry, team or even a generation.

It would come as no surprise if some traits resonated with you more than others. No one person has every single trait, but a marked person certainly has at least half of these traits. There no cookie cutter formulas. I am sure there are some reading this book that have never experienced even half of these traits and are still set apart. This is simply a list. Beyond this list, there should be internal confirmation. What has God said about you? There should be external confirmation. What have others seen on your life? And what fruit have you produced from your life? In other words, what are the extraordinary manifestations that are tangible to those around you? You may be one that is called to change the world and feeling timid right now or broken. You may presently feel misunderstood. You will get there as you uncover who you are. You will get there. For others, you may feel full of courage, faith and boldness. Whatever chapter you are on in this process, the story does not end here.

CHAPTER 2

I Am Marked Now What?

Oftentimes, others see that you are marked for greatness before you do, and when others see that you are unique or different, they begin to treat you differently. It can be tough when you feel something is different about you but you are not sure exactly what it is. The enemy likes to take these feelings of being different and morph them into feelings of rejection or isolation, which makes you hate the very thing that will make you great. Accepting what makes you different is the first step in becoming great. The enemy knows your difference marks you for greatness. People who are called to do something extraordinary do not think like the other people. They are often dreamers, fighters for justice, innovators, creators, deep lovers, and people who simply see life differently. They usually have enormous hope and faith when others don't, and they are brave and courageous when others aren't. While these are great qualities, the enemy's job is to make you hate them and wish you did not feel or see things in a particular way. You will often experience things that will make you want to hate how you think, look, see the world, and how you act. If you can hate yourself, you will not be able to become all God has called you to become.

An Invitation To Authenticity

The journey of authenticity is the process of removing everything else that has shaped our identity but the Holy Spirit. It is the stripping down of expectations and lies which have kept us captive to an image that is not who we really are. We must allow ourselves to know God and to be known by God so He can name us. He desires to tell us what His heart is for our life. When you are gifted or marked, everyone will always want something from you. So the greatest gift you can give yourself is learning who you are outside of people's expectations. A marked person cannot be married to people's expectations and expect to fulfill the call of God on their life. That does not mean we don't care what people say or refuse to take advice from others. It simply means we spend time with the Father and get our validity and our value from Him alone. In order to be authentic, we must be whole.

The journey of authenticity is the journey into wholeness. We need to examine the things in our hearts that are preventing us from becoming who God has called us to be. Is it the fear of man or fear of what people say? Is it low self-esteem? Is it jealousy or comparison? Whatever it is, we must begin the process of getting to the core of it.

Soul Be Made Whole

Below are some suggestions to help you walk out what needs to be healed in the soul. This is a journey I continue to take as God is growing me in His image.

1. **Identify your motives** - Why do you think the way you think? Why do you dress the way you dress? Why do you want to achieve what you want to achieve? Everything we do must be motivated by our love for God, others and ourselves. If anything we do stems from a place of wanting to belong or to be loved or appreciated, we won't be whole and we will not be able to walk in authenticity.

2. **Deal with your identity** – It's imperative to understand that no matter what your background is, what you've been through or where you came from, you are loved by God and you belong to Him. If you have pain in your heart from your mother, father, or people who have hurt you, you must release it. Pain is a hindrance to greatness. Get in a community that understands sonship. Learn from friends who have discovered who they are in God. Go through inner healing prayer. Allow yourself to cry and process everything that hinders you from truly being you. Let go of what could have been, what you have done wrong and who you are not. Celebrate who God is transforming you into. Him. Rely on Him.

3. **Become aware of your weaknesses and celebrate your strengths** – I think of authenticity as the ability to be aware of your weaknesses and

celebrating your strengths. A person who is authentic is aware of what they do well and what they need to work on. They do not run from their weaknesses because they know weakness does not define them. It can help them become better. If you struggle with your identity, with accepting yourself, you will feel like any form of imperfection means you are less than. A mature authentic person says , "Take me as I am. I am aware of what I need to work on and I am also aware of how amazing wonderful I am." As Marianne Williamson says, "There is nothing enlightened about shrinking so that other people won't feel insecure around you. We are all meant to shine, as children do. We were born to make manifest the glory of God that is within us. It's not just in some of us; it's in everyone. And as we let our own light shine, we unconsciously give other people permission to do the same. As we are liberated from our own fear, our presence automatically liberates others."

4. **Give yourself permission to change** - An authentic person does not live by the expectations of others. They live from their expectations of God. This stance allows them to be led by the Holy Spirit. Many people are afraid to become who they know they were made to be because they are afraid of how people will respond. It is your job to become and their job to keep up. Giving yourself permission to grow and change will mean leaving others behind. Becoming what God called you to be may mean stepping out on faith or possibly doing something that has never been done in your family before. It

also means giving yourself permission to grow into who God is calling you to be rather than remaining who you thought you were. Allow yourself to become that person. Marked people are always moving forward. They are creative in nature, set apart, and flexible when it comes to their growth. You can do it. Become who God has called you to be. Part of stepping into the things that God has planned for you is being able to leave the expectations of people behind you. You have to give yourself permission to change and evolve.

5. **Embrace your difference** - Before I knew I was a visionary with the gift to see the future and birth destinies, people said I was weird. As I grew, I realized there was a certain level of expectation from God on my life that others simply did not have. In college, my girlfriends who loved Jesus would go to the club with no issues. I tried it twice and knew I was not supposed to be there. You know it's bad when clubbers come up to you and say, "I do not think you are supposed to be here." These kind of experiences as a young person made me NOT want to be different. I wanted to dance, date different guys, and not feel bad for mistreating someone. I did not want to be different. The problem was when I tried to be normal, I still felt different. Marked people stick out even when they do not want to. I cried out to be normal. But as I grew, I asked myself, "What really is normal? Who sets the standard for normal?" If I am made in the image of God and He created me, then maybe I am the one who is normal and not them.

The enemy has blinded this generation. Many wear a mask and things that are unholy and perverse are deemed normal. Many of us have bought into a lie, and it is really important that we buy into God's truth and God's heart so we can set the standard for what is normal.

Discovering Your People

Another thing that came with being different was that I outgrew people I loved. For some reason, marked people often aspire to grow and evolve at a rate that others do not. As strange as it may seem, everyone is not passionate about doing more or becoming more. Some people are content with how they think, what they are doing, and who they have become. For me, being different mandated that I change my environment and the people in it. Sometimes often. It wasn't that I was better than anyone else, I just saw life from a different perspective. As a result, most of the time I only had a small group of friends, and I have learned that's okay. Though I was always popular because of my sanguine temperament, there were times I felt left out even in the in-crowd. This dissonance, the pressure of not understanding why your life works and looks differently from everyone else's life and relationships, was hard.

As I grew in God, there where seasons of fruitfulness and joy while running with worshipping, prophetic, and a pioneering set of friends like me. They understood my wit, determination and passion for Jesus. I felt at home, until the vision on my life started to expand and the Lord began calling me to more. When my audience and the way I approached ministry changed, I was ostracized by those I thought were just like me. And once again I found myself back at that place—different and alone. Every stretch in God will require some shedding in the process. You cannot stretch in tight quarters. The perimeters created by others or yourself must extend or burst. This time, some of them busted. Once again, I questioned myself, my steps forward, and what I thought God was calling me to. I wrestled with this idea of being marked and why it had such a high price.

One thing you must know that this process of walking with others and then walking alone is cycle. You will have seasons of flourishing friendships and seasons with less friendships and a call from God to go higher or deeper in Him.

CHAPTER 3

Marked And Prophetic

When we speak of the prophetic ministry, R. Loren Sandford has this to say to you, "You are not alone." In his book, *Understanding Prophetic People,* Sandford compiled a profile of the traits of prophetic people. This profile helps to identify traits of prophetic people, however it does not guarantee that having these traits means you are prophetic. What they do offer are clues into people who are set apart.

Prophetic people come from all backgrounds and all walks of life. Some are simple and ordinary. Some stand out and are known by people all over the world. One of the things you will notice as we go through some of these traits is the more they resonate with you, the more likely it is that you are called into the office of a prophet not merely a prophetic gift.

Sandford begins with the **"Temperamental Eccentric" trait.** He shares how historically, prophets such as Ezekiel acted strangely by baking bread using cow manure (Eze. 4:15) while Hosea married a prostitute against conventional wisdom. When a person does not know that they are a prophetic, this trait may show up in how they dress. They may be extremely burdened by societal ills. They may want to push the envelope and decry being normal or following the status quo.

They are the thinkers, creatives, misfits. The difficulty a misfit has is that they feel like they are on their own. They have no sense of purpose and often feel like the world is conspiring against them. An eccentric person will finally feel settled in who they are when they discover their identity in the Father and understand that God has wired and created them to be unique.

Loren Sandford also mentions a temperamental trait. Merriam Webster defines temperamental as "a : marked by excessive sensitivity and impulsive mood changes b : unpredictable in behavior or performance." Scripture is very clear that gifts and calling come without repentance (Romans 11:29). The gift of prophecy and the function or grace as a prophet is one that we are born with. Until we are aware of this, many of the things we see, sense or hear are going to be very difficult for us to interpret or explain. Those with the prophetic gift may feel other people's burden. This may be felt in the prophetic person's heart or as a heaviness around them. Prophetic types can hear or see other people's pain or conditions. The point of this is, first and foremost, to serve as intercessors for those people in pain and if directed by the Lord, share with them what we are sensing or feeling. Prophetic people become temperamental when they do not know how to manage what they are hearing seeing or sensing. They often feel like what they feel is their own feelings, when it's quite possible they are moody because they're feeling the pain of someone in their environment. It is very important that prophetic people learn how to differentiate their feelings and their moods so they can learn to balance their emotions.

Many have ended up with mental health diagnosis or felt as if they were going crazy due to a lack of training and teaching on the difference between internal voices, the voice of God and other factors attempting to speak to them.

As shared in the previous chapters, many marked people go through "wilderness" experiences. This is a season in which the Lord molds your character, humbling and breaking off anything that does not glorify Him. Sandford goes on to say that this process may take on the form of a "wilderness" whereby the prophetic person's life is marked by setbacks, rejection, humiliation, persecution, deep personal loss, etc. This constant "crucifixion" of the flesh and "suffering" of the soul are essential to the prophetic calling. This type of crushing may seem incomprehensible to the average Christian and puzzling even to the prophetic person. But this is the place where the anointing is poured out; the fear of man is broken and total dependence on the Father is birthed. Instead of letting this become a place of turmoil or confusion, if we submit to God, it will become a place of surrender and submission.

During the wilderness season God will allow you to have supernatural experiences and encounters, but the enemy wants you to hold these to yourself. He tells you lies like "No one will understand," or "You are losing your mind." Just know many have walked this road before. Even if you feel you have no one to share these experiences with, speak to God about them. Journal. Write a song. Find a way to express your experiences. Do not withdraw from friends or family just because they do not understand you. Find ways to connect beyond the experiences you are having. Sandford states many times the Lord uses this season in the "wilderness" to break, humble, refine and instill tenacity in the prophetic person so they may withstand the lust of the flesh, the lust of the eye and the pride of life (1 John 2:16). God has a great and expected end for you marked on. You might be in the middle of the process where nothing makes sense, but better is the end of a thing than the beginning. It will all work out.

Chapter 4

Growing Confident In God's Voice

Many of the hardships we walk through is due to a lack of confidence in God's voice. It is imperative that a marked person understand the way God communicates with them and walks in it. It will help you discern seasons, friendships and God's heart towards you. God speaks to you based on your temperament and personality. He can use your favorite song, a walk in the park or a piece of art to convey His heart to you. Below I share some conventional ways in which God communicates. Most marked people have experienced some or many of these. Our communication with God should grow as we grow in Him.

The Prophetic Ministry

What is prophecy? Is it still alive today? Why do believers need to be able to hear the Lord, discern spirits, seasons and times? How do you use prophecy as a tool for evangelism?

God is releasing His glory on the earth. He is calling us to walk in a higher revelation of Him and in all the gifting of the Holy Spirit so that we can be a part of the end time harvest and help equip the body of Christ for His return. I believe it is God's heart that we are able to perceive what He is saying and apply it to our lives and into the lives of others. Many churches shy away from prophecy or the prophetic because of lack of knowledge, abuse of the gift and other misunderstandings. However, we are in a time where God is speaking more and more. We need to understand why He is speaking to us and what to do with what He is saying. My simplest definition of prophecy is perceiving what God is saying and applying it to yourself, others or the nations.

As the time for Jesus to return draws near, the need for us to be able to discern and understand what is happening is going to be very important. Throughout the Old Testament, God spoke through prophets. Kings consulted prophets. Generals in armies consulted prophets and ordinary people consulted prophets.

The prophets were people God had chosen to be able to perceive what He was saying or doing so that they could help lead the people of Israel. God is doing the same in our day. He is raising more and more prophetic voices to help people discern and know what the perfect will of God is for their lives.

1 Corinthians 14:1 states, "Pursue love, and desire spiritual gifts, but especially that you may prophesy." Paul says this because prophecy is a gift everyone can benefit from. I have seen the prophetic ministry set people free, bring clarity, and propel people into their destinies. I have seen countless people breakdown saying "I was just praying that today," or "I really thought I was crazy, but you have confirmed everything I was seeing," or "I did not know what I do until now." God is so good! He wants to speak to His children. He wants to help us. This is why He speaks to us so we can speak into to other people's lives.

Prophecy is for the edification of the body, which means building up, exhorting (encouraging) and comforting (1 Corinthians 14:3-4). When someone speaks a prophetic word into your life it should build you up in some way. Even if it's a warning to turn away from sin, it should be for the purpose of building that person up not exposing them. One of my favorite prophetic teachers Graham Cooke says, "God speaks to the treasure not the earthen vessels." Some people have the notion that prophetic people can see everything even the bad in people-- this is not true. When God shows a prophetic person a word of correction, in an effort to build the other person up and set them free from whatever is hindering them, they should deliver the word to in love.

Prophecy should encourage. Encourage you to believe that God really loves you and sees you. Encourage you to keep walking in faith. Encourage you to believe God's purposes for your life. Encourage you to do the right thing. An exhortative prophetic word is a word that strongly urges you to stay on a course or pursue new direction.

Prophecy should comfort you. I have received some of the most comforting words when I most needed them through the prophetic ministry. Some of them have been as simple as "God loves you" or "God thinks you are beautiful." While these may seem simple to some people, these words can change someone's whole day and possibly, their life. These types of prophetic comforting words lets us know that God is with us and that He sees us.

Prophecy is when a person can perceive what God is saying or doing and is able to apply it to his or her own life or reveal it to another person to help them in their life. Prophecy is for the edification, exhortation and comfort of the body. Prophecy is a tool to help bring unbelievers into the body of Christ and is also used to warn nations, churches, to declare God's plans, to give direction, and to activate faith, but the purpose of this chapter is to gain practical understanding of what prophecy is and how to use it in ministry.

Can We All Prophesy?

The prophetic ministry can be broken down into three categories: the spirit of prophecy, the gift of prophecy and the office of a prophet. The following definitions are not exhaustive definitions but they will give us a better understanding of the prophetic ministry.

Spirit Of Prophecy

There is a level of prophecy that is for everyone in the body of Christ. 1 Corinthians 14: 1-5 makes that clear. "Pursue love, and desire spiritual gifts, but especially that you may prophecy. For he who speaks in a tongue does not speak to men but to God, for no one understands him; however, in the spirit he speaks mysteries. But he who prophesies speaks edification and exhortation and comfort to men. He who speaks in a tongue edifies himself, but he who prophesies edifies the church. I wish you all spoke with tongues, but even more that you prophesy."

Paul says he wishes that all would prophesy. I believe that God speaks to everyone and everyone hears and perceives Him differently. God does this so we can all edify and comfort one another in our churches and in the body of Christ. We may not all reveal what God has said the same way, but we can all share a word of encouragement from a dream, an impression, or the word of God to the body of Christ and people in our communities. Paul says desire this spiritual gift, which implies that some may not initially have the gift, but God can give it to them. And I believe the more we use it to bless others, the more God entrusts us with more of His love and revelation for others around us.

The prophetic anointing is magnified when you get around other prophetic people. In1 Samuel 19, Saul sent a group of men to find David who was being hidden by Samuel the prophet. As the men neared the city, they began to prophesy. Two more groups were dispatched and they too began to prophesy when they got close to the city. After this, Saul decided to go to the city himself, and he too prophesied. So goes the saying, "Is Saul also among the prophets?" This is a great example of the spirit of prophecy.

In many churches or nations where the leaders are prophetic, various people in the churches easily walk in the prophetic. Great examples of these types of churches are Bethel Church in Redding, California, and Morningstar in Fort Mill, South Carolina. The spirit of prophecy is for the body of Christ to be able to exhort, edify and comfort one another. You can pray for that gift right now so that you may prophesy. It is given to the body and all individuals can operate in it from time to time as the Spirit gives unction.

Gift Of Prophecy

The gift of prophecy is one of the twelve spiritual gifts. The purpose of this gift is the same as the spirit of prophecy. However, this is given to certain people in the body by the Holy Spirit. The Holy Spirit gives it to whomever He wills, just like any other gift (e.g. healing or the gift of faith). In my experience, these are people who can easily hear from the Lord and reveal the Lord's plan at any point. The people with these gifts are usually the ones you can go to and ask for prayer and they can easily speak into your life. These people also hear from the Lord through dreams, visions, and other supernatural encounters. They are positioned in a ministry or church body to encourage and build up their church and community. This gift is the same as the other gifts such as faith, healing, wisdom etc. Again, God gives those gifts to the body by the Holy Spirit however He pleases.

Office Of The Prophet

This third level in the prophetic is probably the most controversial office in the body of Christ. I am not sure why because the Bible clearly says in Ephesians 4:11-12, "And he gave some, apostles; and some, prophets; and some, evangelists; and some, pastors and teachers; For the perfecting of the saints, for the work of the ministry, for the edifying of the body of Christ." The prophetic office is just as alive today as it was in the Old Testament. God has given the body of Christ apostles, prophets, evangelists, pastors and teachers for the perfecting of the saints. Prophets are spoken about in the New Testament, especially in the book of Acts (Acts 11:27-30; 13:1; 15:32; 19:6).

The office of the prophet has been feared because abuse has occurred in the past. But that does not mean the office does not exist. Many denominations believe in pastors, evangelist and teachers but are leery when it comes to prophets and apostles. We are living in a day where we cannot pick and choose what we want from the Bible. We must believe in the full gospel and every gift that God has given to His body.

People who are called to the prophetic office have a mandate over their lives to declare what the Lord has given them over people, churches, city, and nations. Prophets in the Old and New Testament were used to warn nations and kings about impeding danger and to share the heart of the Lord to the people. Prophets stand for righteousness. God gives them a particular issue such as repentance or righteousness to stand on and declare. John the Baptist declared the way of the Lord in the New Testament. Moses was a mouthpiece to help set the captives free in the Old Testament. Deborah was a prophetess who sat and brought counsel to a nation and led generals to battle. Jeremiah, Isaiah and Ezekiel all carried a burden for the nation of Israel, serving as God's mouthpiece to that nation. Even today, God has risen up prophetic mouthpieces to the nations. Lou Engle is an example of a present-day prophet whose whole life, in my opinion, exemplifies the burden the

Lord has put on him. Cindy Jacobs and Cindy Trimm are both women with huge prophetic mantles.

When you are called to the office of a prophet, it is beyond prophesying to some people here and there. The Lord gives you a burden for a particular issue. The Lord has given Lou Engle a burden for social justice and the abolishment of slavery. There are also times when the Lord gives you specific regions, nations or people groups to release words over and intercede for. The prophetic office is not one you can pick up and put down. It is who you are. It is important to note that there are real live prophets today. Not only do those in the prophetic office need to have a proven record of prophesying accurately, they should exhibit fruits of love, holiness and righteousness. You shall know them by their fruit.

Mechanics Of Prophecy

The last part of this book will discuss how people hear from God and the mechanics of prophesying. But before I cover the ways we hear from the Lord, I want to cover the some questions novices in the prophetic always ask me.

How do I know it is the Lord speaking to me?

The answer is simple. Ask yourself these three things. Does this line up with scripture? Who does this glorify? Me or my flesh, the enemy, or God? If the answer is yes to the first two, then pray on it or seek counsel. If it is God, then go ahead a release that word. If you are still unsure, seek help from a mentor or a leader.

It is so important for prophetic people to be surrounded by other prophetic people for the sake of wise counsel. As the proverbs says, "there is safety in a multitude of counselors." The last question you want to ask yourself is *does the prophetic word edify, comfort or exhort those for whom it is intended?* If you can answer yes to this, then you know it is the voice of the Lord speaking to you.

What if I am wrong? How do I know if it is God?

If it is going to edify, comfort or exhort another person, then what do you have to lose? Even if it is a simple, "Jesus loves you," go ahead and share it. That is a word of exhortation. Sometimes what the Lord shares with us may not make much sense to us, but when you give it to the person it makes sense to them. It is not for us to figure out the meaning of the word, it is for us to deliver it. We are mere mouthpieces, messengers. We just deliver the word and the people choose what to do with it, which brings me to a very important point.

It is very important to practice your prophetic gift in a safe setting. Find a place where you can make mistakes and have people correct you in love and help you grow, places like a small prayer group or Bible study where the leaders can work with you. I started ministering through my prophetic gift in a Bible study where the people knew me and knew I had been called to this ministry. They had a lot of grace and so did the Lord. He loved my obedience and my desire to learn. You have to have a teachable spirit in this ministry because there is a lot to learn. God is trusting us with His heart in order for us to share it with other people and we cannot take it for granted.

Here is a nugget for you: the more you obey and the quicker you obey, the more the Lord is going to trust you with what He has given you. The first step in prophesying is taking the step. Share what you are sensing, seeing, hearing or dreaming. You will be surprised at how much of a blessing you will be to another life.

CHAPTER 5

Mastering your Dialogue with God

There are several ways that God has wired us to hear from Him. The first way is through *impressions*. This is the lowest and most prevalent way of hearing from the Lord. An impression is a sudden knowing that is pressed upon your heart either about yourself or someone you are to minister to. Each one of us, at one time or another, have said, "Something told me to do that," or "I just felt like that was the way to go." That little something is the Holy Spirit. God speaks to us by impressing something in our spirits. The world calls it intuition, I call it Jesus. It is hard sometimes to discern that little voice or that impression because it is the same as our own thought or voice. The voice of the Lord brings peace and calmness. If you hear a voice and it leaves you confused or frustrated, it is either yourself or the enemy. The presence of the Lord is peaceable. "For you will go out with joy and be led forth with peace" (Isaiah 55:12). Every believer has impressions. They are the first level of discernment. When one is able to learn how to recognize that the impression is from the Lord and obey it, then God begins to release other prophetic giftings. Impressions are inborn in all humans. They help us know what is right and wrong. It is the Holy Spirit in us guiding us and giving us directions.

The second way we hear from the Lord is by **hearing.** Similar to what we discussed in the previous chapter, the voice of God is calm and peaceable, and it will most likely sound like your own voice. However, there are times when we might hear the "audible" voice of God. This is a literal external audible voice that one hears. This way of hearing from the Lord is rare and usually when it happens to a person, it is terrifying. It is the actual voice of almighty God speaking to you. This happened to me on one occasion, and I literally fell to ground under the power of the Holy Spirit. In the Bible, Moses heard the voice of God speaking to him at the burning bush.

It is important to follow the guidelines we learned in the previous chapter about discerning the voice of God. John 10:4-5 states, ".... and his sheep follow him because they know his voice. But they will never follow a stranger; in fact, they will run away from him because they do not recognize a stranger's voice." We must learn his voice and know his voice. At the end of this chapter, I will discuss ways to walk in the prophetic and one of them is being a friend of God, being intimate with God and knowing His voice. When we learn His voice, we can easily follow after Him and understand all He is saying to us.

The third way to we hear from God is through **seeing**. There are several ways that we "see" what the Lord is saying. The most common is through dreams. Everyone dreams. The key is learning how to discern which dreams are from God, which ones are soulish and which ones are from the enemy. Dreams are all over the Bible. The coming of Jesus in the Gospels all describe countless times in which angels and the Lord himself spoke through dreams and visions. The Book of Daniel is also filled with dreams. Some dreams are easy to interpret and some are more complex. The same rules we have applied to understanding impressions and hearing can be utilized in the way of dreams. Though dreams are very intricate, God wants us to seek Him for the interpretation. He also has gifted many people in the body to help in the interpretation of dreams. At the end of this book I have included some books that help you grow in the prophetic and dream interpretation. I suggest reading some of the ones I have suggested on dream interpretation and dreams.

The next level of seeing is through **visions**. You can have open visions, which means your eyes are open and you are seeing things through your mind's eye or the eyes of your heart. It appears as if you are watching a movie or seeing a still picture from a camera. Either way, the picture is there in front of you. An example of this is in Acts 10:3 when the angel of the Lord appeared to Cornelius in a vision. Visions are usually distinct and clear.

John Paul Jackson once said, "Visions are direct messages and dreams usually require us seeking the heart of God to get a clearer understanding of what He wants us to see." Benny Hinn said the clearer a dream or vision, the more urgent. The less clarity, the more time you have to figure it out.

Another way of seeing is through a trance. It is a state in which you are neither awake nor asleep that the Lord begins to speak to you. This happens a lot to me when I am about to fall asleep. Peter fell into a trance in Acts 10:10. It is like a dream while you are awake or a vision so real you feel like you are a part of it.

The fourth way you can hear from God is through **angels**. This is one of those controversial areas in the church. Once again, there are countless examples of angels bringing messages to the children of God in the Bible—in the book of Daniel, as well as Luke 1:26 when the angel of the Lord appeared to Mary about the coming of Jesus. As believers, we must know that angels will never ask you to worship them. They will never ask you to do anything contrary to the word of God. If they do, you need to rebuke them because they are angels of darkness masquerading as angels of light.

The fifth way the Lord speaks to us is through His **Word.** The Word of God, the Holy Bible, is full of prophecies. It is full of exhortations, edifications and warnings of what is to come. God will speak to you through scripture verses for your personal edification or others. Let us never place the word of God above any other gift of the Spirit. His Word comes to instruct, correct, edify and encourage us.

The final way to hear from God is by Jesus himself coming to speak with you. An example of this is in Acts 23:10-11 when Jesus comes to encourage Paul. Jesus may appear to us in dreams or in visions. Others have actually seen him just as some have actually heard his audible voice.

I remember when I was eleven or twelve, laying in the bed in a trance like state and Jesus appeared to me and reached out His hand. I was so excited and thought everyone at youth group would be too. But they just thought I was strange. God does appear to us to comfort or warn us or just let us know that He is near.

Now that you know about the prophetic, the different levels of the prophetic, and how we hear from

God, it is important to know the keys for developing and maintaining a prophetic lifestyle. Hearing from God is a gift given to us in different measures but all those measures can be increased through intimacy with the Father. The Bible says in Amos 3 that He never does anything without giving warning to the prophets his servants or in some versions, his friends. In the next section, we will discuss how to grow in the prophetic and maintain our ability to hear from God.

Keys To A Prophetic Lifestyle

God is looking for friends. He is looking for servants He can share His heart with. He is looking for people who will hear His voice and obey. Every Christian is called to walk in a measure of the prophetic in that they are called to hear God's voice and be able to encourage and bless others.

When people ask me how did you become prophetic? I say, "I prayed." To clarify, I know this is a gifting from God. But beyond gifting, we must understand that intimacy and friendship with Jesus is the number one goal. Prophetic people should be, first of all, intercessors. We must understand the art of prayer, the discipline of communing with God, and the delight of abiding with Him. One of my life verses is John chapter 14:11, "I am in the father and the father is in me. Together we bear much fruit." The body of Christ must understand that Jesus wants intimacy, and out of that, every other gifting flows— prophecy, working of signs and wonders or healing. If we seek to know God's heart, we will be moved by compassion to be a blessing to his people. We must develop lifestyles of worship in everything we do. Whether we eat or drink, whatever we do, let us do it unto the Lord (1 Corinthians 10:32). We must acknowledge Him in all we do.

Lastly, we must learn to love. 1 Corinthians 13:2 states, "If I have the gift of prophecy and can fathom all mysteries and all knowledge, and if I have a faith that can move mountains, but have not love, I am nothing." If we do not prophecy out of love for others and love for God, we are nothing. Everything Jesus did, He did with compassion (Matthew 9:36, Matthew 20:34). We prophecy not to be seen or heard, we prophesy because we love and we desire the people of God to know the will and heart of God for their lives. We must always walk in humility because we are mere vessels. We are earthen vessels with treasures in us so that the excellency of power may be of God and not ourselves (1 Corinthians 4:7). He has filled us with His glorious light. Let it shine before men so they will turn and glorify the Lord above (1 Peter 2:12). Trust Him with your heart. Let Him speak to you and allow Him to minister to you. As you develop that relationship, He will release gifts in you so that you can share them with the rest of the world.

CHAPTER 6

What am I marked for?

Simple Questions to help you discover Purpose

These are simple questions that I normally take my coaching clients through to help them come to this conclusion. I hope they will lead you to more clarity and more confidence in who God is calling you to become.

1. A) What makes you feel alive? B) Think about three to five things that brings you joy and makes you feel energetic. C) What one or two things do you love to do and would do even if no one paid you to do them? D) What is the one thing that no matter how tired you are, once you have done it you feel energy and purpose?

Write your answers below:

A._____

B_____

C. _____

D._____

2. A)What breaks your heart or makes you angry? What makes your blood boil? B)What makes you cry? C)What burdens your heart concerning the world and people? D)What kind of news stories keep you up at night?

Write your answers below:

A._____

B_____

C. _____

D._____

3. A)What if there were no limitations? If money, education, time, or resources were not limiting you, what would you be doing with your life? B)Where would you go? C)Whose lives would you change? D)What broken thing would you fix?

Write your answers below:

A._____

B_____

C. _____

D._____

4. Family Matters - Many people do not realize that our family carries certain traits and genes to help us excel in our purpose. Are there any areas of occupation, interest, or skills that a lot of your family have? For example, do you come from a line of teachers, pastors, or artists? List two or three occupations below.

*** For some this question is hard because they may not know their family or most of the careers the family chose were out of necessity and not necessarily passion. If you come from a background like that, feel free to skip this question or write the best answer possible.*

5. What have you been named? What prophetic words have you received about your life? For example, has someone prophesied that you're going to be a teacher or you're going to be a great mother? If you have not received any prophetic words, what do people call you? For example, do they say you're a good listener or you are innovative or strong? What are some of the things you have been named? List them below.

_____

_____

_____

Let's take your answers and craft a fuller prophetic picture. Question one refers to the tools that you've been given to change the world. Perhaps you feel most alive when you are singing, teaching, cooking, reading or dancing. These are clues about what you've been made to do to change the world. Your answers to question two offers clues into what you're going to change. A person does not find meaning until they find a problem to solve, so the things that break your heart or make you angry are part of what you are supposed to solve. You need to figure out how to partner with what makes you feel alive to help you solve number two. I feel most alive when I am teaching, counseling or coaching others, and my heart breaks when people don't know who God has called them to be or when people don't have clear sense of their identity. Through my coaching, counseling, writing and teaching, I help people discover identity and purpose.

The answers to question three should lead you to what you are truly made to do and it should intersect with your answers to questions one and two. Question four speaks to a skill that is already within you, one that you have probably already identified in your answers to question one or two. If your family is passionate about justice or working with broken people, you may have the same passion. Your answers to question five will likely confirm what has already been in your heart. Usually, we are already doing most of the things people say we are or the things that are prophesied to us. If not, deep down, we know that's who we are. How do we become the culmination of all these things that are in our hearts? I'm glad you asked.

CHAPTER 7

Becoming What You Marked For

One of the greatest battles for people marked for greatness is a battle against themselves. They constantly struggle with an array of emotions that if not dealt with can cost them their destiny.

The Longing For Belonging–

We all want to be accepted. We all want to belong, but as I have previously mentioned in the earlier chapters, there will be seasons where you do not fit in, where you just do not belong. However, you need to remember there will be somewhere you do fit in. Do not get so used to not belonging that you always see yourself on the outside when you really are not. God puts us in families. When you come to understand that, you will seek out friendships. You will draw your people to you. Even in our quirkiness or difference, you were made to belong, and you will belong.

People who are called to do great things think differently. They are often ahead of the curve, and you can start to feel peace being alone. It's imperative to look for those who are for you. Remember on those tough nights, you belong in the kingdom of God and in that family, you will always be understood and you will always have a place. Take time to get to know yourself, what you need and what you are looking for. When you are clear about that, God will highlight those who have been with you all along.

Lone Ranger Complex

With that said, just because you may not always belong does not mean you have to be alone. God has a tribe for you, a group of people that understand you. Sometimes it is just one best friend and sometimes it is a whole community. The greatest hinderance to achieving great things for God is the decision to do things alone. I know people may not get you. I know you may have been hurt. Instead of allowing the enemy to isolate you so you do not accomplish what God has called you to do, find ones like yourself and change the world together. There is nothing you have been called to do that you will be able to accomplish without help. As the old African proverb says, "If you want to go fast, go alone. If you want to go far, go together."

Going alone can help you go fast, but what God has called you to requires that you go with someone. Different seasons will bring different people into your life. We marked ones need people. We need community. God's dream for our lives intentionally requires that we deal with our friendship issues and any other relational issues we have, whether from previous experiences or perceived interactions.

Overcoming Rejection

Based on their experiences in life or things that have been done to them, marked people may struggle with abandonment or rejection. Here are ten ways to assess if you are struggling with rejection.

1. **You tend to reject others before they can reject you** - You tend to believe that at some point or another, people will leave you, betray you or hurt you. So, before you even give them a chance, you push them away to avoid experiencing pain.

2. **You punish people when they leave you** - You tend to stop talking to people when they leave you, tell others to stop talking to them or carry unforgiveness towards the person who left.

3. **You feel pity for yourself or entitled** - People that struggle with rejection often feel like they have been dealt the worst cards and oftentimes want others to treat them in a special way. The pity they demand drains friendships and the sense of entitlement pushes people away.

4. **You struggle with pride** - You are okay with helping and taking care of others but have difficulty receiving help or care from others.

5. **You do not like to be corrected** - To a person who struggles with rejection, correction is viewed as an assault against that person's identity and not the thing they did wrong. People who struggle with

rejection have a hard time separating what people are asking from themselves.

6. **You internalize** – You take on what others say and do and somehow connect it to your own issues or identity, often blaming external events on yourself even if it has nothing to do with you.

7. **Difficulty with authority** - People struggling with rejection often have a hard time listening or taking orders. They may be blunt in their resistance or passive aggressive if unable to assert their independence and individuality.

8. **Fabricated personalities** - You will find that when someone struggles with abandonment or rejection they tend to take on the personalities of the people they want to be accepted by. This often causes them to change their personality based on the people they are with, fabricating whatever personality they think people will love. This results in confusion and double minded lifestyle.

9. **Jealousy, envy, and comparison** - When a marked person is unable to love themselves, they will never see themselves as enough, constantly comparing their and skills to others.

10. **Sabotage** - Marked people sometimes develop mechanisms that end up sabotaging what they are working to build. When people have experienced betrayal or rejection, they tend to make subconscious decisions that will only allow them to get so far before they mess things up. People used

to chaos or failure tend to repeat that cycle in their relationships and lives because it is what feels normal. Marked people can be close to breakthrough and somehow manage to destroy the very opportunity they have been believing for. This can happen in friendships as well as our own emotional health. It's important to identify how you think and the areas in which you need to grow so you are not the cause of your lack of progression.

Lack of Character

Character is developed in the mundane things that don't draw a lot of attention or hype. If God can trust us to be a people of our word, to complete tasks, to always tell the truth, to be a loyal friend, He can trust us to lead many. Oftentimes, people of great destiny have to master small things before they can walk into great things. When you are marked, it is even harder because God may have you repeat things or go through things that others do not. The whole story of Joseph, and many other marked people, going through the process is for one main purpose — our ability to love God, trust God and love others. Character is everything, particularly for marked people who are often very gifted but not yet mature in conduct and love. We must make character more of a priority than trying to become someone great.

Poor Choices In Relationships

Our emotional stability and stamina is greatly influenced by those around us. The enemy works really hard to make us have experiences that either cause us to be unable to choose wisely when it comes to relationships or develop bad habits that attract negative people into our life. When you are marked, your friendships and relationships are one of the greatest indicators of you becoming who God has called you to become. Due to our struggle to be affirmed, valued, and loved, marked people often accept unhealthy people into their lives. We attract people who suck the life out of us, and we tend to compromise and dumb ourselves down because of the insecurities around us. Look for people who are honest about your greatness yet patient and able to help you heal and repair your broken parts. Seek relationships in which both parties are growing and learning. You deserve life giving friendships that patient with you and willing to fight for you.

Fear

One of the greatest tools the enemy uses against marked ones is fear. Fear of what others will think or say. Fear of failure or the fear of actually succeeding. The truth is you are afraid because the enemy is afraid of you finding out who you really are. His greatest fear is that you realize how amazing you are, how set apart you are. All he does is create a series of events to cause you to come out of agreement with God's plans and come into agreement with his lies. You must remember that you have an enemy and his job is to rob you of your inheritance. Fear is a thief. If you know you are walking with God and you have a great crowd of those who have gone before you cheering you on, you will learn to overcome obstacles while afraid. It is okay to feel fear from time to time, but it is not okay to allow it to limit you from becoming all God called you to be. Remember fear paralyzes and faith propels. You were made to leave a mark. Go do it!

Book List

Dreams:

"Understanding the dreams you dreams" – Ira Milligan

"The Divinity Code understanding your dreams"- Adam Thompson and Adrian Beale

"Dream Language"- James Goll

Unlocking your Dreams- Autumn Mann

Apostles and Apostolic Ministry:

Apostles Today by C. Peter Wagner

The Gift of the Apostle by David Cannistraci

Eternity's Generals- Dr. Paula Price

50 truths concerning Apostolic Ministry- John Eckhardt

Moving in the Apostolic- John Eckhardt

Aligning with the Apostolic- Dr Bruce Cook

Apostles Prophets and the Coming Moves of God-Dr Bill Hamon

Apostles Then and Now-Mark Pfeifer

The Apostolic Ministry-Rick Joyner

The Ministry of the Apostle-Guillermo Maldonado

Prophets and the Prophetic Ministry:

The Prophets Dictionary-Dr Paula Price

The Prophet's Handbook- Dr Paula Price

Faith Wokoma- Prophecy 101

Prophecy-God's Communication Media

Basic Training for Prophetic Ministry-Kris Vallotton

Thus Saith the Lord? John Bevere

The Prophetic Ministry-Frank Damazio

Approaching the heart of prophecy-Graham Cooke

The ABCs of Prophecy-Elexio Baillou

The Seer-Jim Goll

God Still Speaks-John Eckhardt

Growing in the Prophetic-Mike Bickle

Prophecy and Responsibility-Graham Cooke

Prophets and Personal Prophecy-Dr. Bill Hamon

Prophets and Prophetic Pitfalls-Dr. Bill Hamon

Prophets and the Prophetic Movement-Dr. Bill Hamon

Purifying the Prophetic- R. Loren Sandford

Prophetic Ministry-Rick Joyner

School of the Prophets-Kris Vallotton

Secrets of the Prophetic- Kim Clement

Translating God-Shawn Bolz

Understanding Your Personal Prophecy-Gary Cake

The Voice of God-Cindy Jacobs

School of the Seers-Jonathan Welton

New Covenant Prophetic Ministry- Jim and Carolyn Welton

User-Friendly Prophecy-Larry Randolph

Elijah's Revolution-Jim Goll

Fivefold Ministry:

Divine Order for Spiritual Dominance-Dr Paula Price

The Fivefold Ministry Offices- Dr Paula Price

Fivefold Ministry Made Practical-Dr Paula Price

Discover Your Spiritual Gifts-C. Peter Wagner

Understanding the Fivefold Ministry-Matthew Green .

Destiny/Supernatural living:

"When Heaven Invades Earth" – Bill Johnson"

"The Matriarchal Dimension: Positioning Spiritual Mothers and Prophetic Women fo rDestiny" – Dr. Keira Taylor-Banks

When heaven opens-Discovering the power of Devine encounters"- Graham Cooke and Lucas Sherraden

"Answering your call: A Guide for living your deepest purpose"- John P Schuster

"Celebration of Discipline"- Richard J. Foster

BIBLIOGRAPHY

2007. SANDFORD, L. R., UNDERSTANDING PROPHETIC PEOPLE: BLESSINGS AND PROBLEMS OF PROPHETIC PEOPLE. BAKER PUBLISHING GROUP

Made in the USA
Monee, IL
29 August 2021

76175778R00039